A Narrative Rewritten

a collection of personal writings for adult survivors of childhood incest & sexual abuse

Michaia Walker

Gotham Books

30 N Gould St.
Ste. 20820, Sheridan, WY 82801
https://gothambooksinc.com/

Phone: 1 (307) 464-7800

© 2025 *Michaia Walker*. All rights reserved.

No part of this book may be reproduced, stored in a retrieval system, or transmitted by any means without the written permission of the author.

Published by Gotham Books (March 27, 2025)

ISBN: 979-8-3492-4067-6 (P)
ISBN: 979-8-3492-4068-3 (E)

Because of the dynamic nature of the Internet, any web addresses or links contained in this book may have changed since publication and may no longer be valid.

The views expressed in this work are solely those of the author and do not necessarily reflect the views of the publisher, and the publisher hereby disclaims any responsibility for them.

Foreword

This originally started out as a project for me to write myself alive in 2015 as part of an online bootcamp. My goal for it was to help me heal from a childhood of traumatic experiences. It morphed into something much bigger as I wrote and shared my writings with others. This book is for anyone who can identify with what has been written. I sincerely hope you get as much out of this book as I was able to express. This book is about healing. Over and over again.

Each poem and reflection is placed in a particular order. I want my readers to make as much meaning of them as they desire but I wanted to explain the format briefly. This book transitions from hurt to healing to hope for the future. It is very raw and potentially triggering (TW: detailed mentions of sexual molestation and suicidality). Most of the poems can stand alone but in this compilation they serve as a stepping stone from one part to the next. From "Bizarre Ones" to "Alchemy" this book is a journey into the deepest parts of my soul that hopefully will resonate with yours.
I wrote this book in 2015 initially and I have the great honor of being able to republish this edited version with the lived experience of an additional 10 years to draw from. There was so much shame in me when I first published this book. I used a pseudonym and only told a handful of people that felt safe to me. At the time, I was significantly short-sighted and did not want to be associated with something so vulnerable and

raw because I thought it would change other people's opinion of me or make them think I was broken or sick.

To my amazement, each time I shared this with a person, my demonstration of vulnerability was received and held. As I learned more about myself and my identities these last 9 years, I have been able to access the hope and healing I wrote about and craved in 2015. If I could go back to that version of me, I would tell them to keep going and keep their heart open to all the love that is on the way.

People will sometimes tell you not to talk about things that make you feel pain. They will tell you to forget and to move on. However, healing does not occur when trying to just forget or and remove that subject from your vocabulary. Things that cause us pain need to be talked about so that we may fully externalize them from ourselves, process them and set them aside. You can't move on from something you carry within yourself. No one benefits when you stuff things down. Least of all you.

Deepest thanks to my dear friend Peter for contributing your amazing skills and creative mind to illustrate this book. This has been a very special project to work on together. Thank you for holding a safe space for me.

"It's up to the artist: writer, painter, musician, to create.
It's up to the audience: reader, viewer, listener, to make it meaningful."

-Michaia Walker

Table of Contents

PART 1: HURTING 1
   1. Bizarre Ones 3
   2. A Narrative Rewritten 4
   3. A Letter to my Molester 5
   4. Depression 7
   5. Hard 10
   6. Suicidal 10
   7. Tears 11

PART 2: HEALING 13
   1. Let's Be Honest 15
   2. Best 17
   3. Can't Love 18
   4. Demons 19
   5. Come Inside 20

Part 3: HOPE 21
   1. Vulnerability 23
   2. Need 25
   3. Hold me 26
   4. "I Love You"--A Dream 28
   5. Don't Get Used to Me 29
   6. Home 30
   7. Breathe 31
   8. Alchemy 32

PART 1: HURTING

Content Warning: The following section contains explicit description of sexual assault and suicidality.
If you or someone you know is struggling with feelings of self-harm and/or suicidal ideation or behavior, *please* reach out for help. See below for some resources.

Crisis Text Line: Text GO to 741741
Suicide Prevention Hotline: (800) 273-TALK or text 988 (available 24 hours a day)
Trans Lifeline: (877) 565-8860
Call Blackline: (800) 604-5841 (Prioritizes BIPOC)
NYC: 1-888-NYC-Well (1-888-692-9355), or text "WELL" to 65173
Trevor Project: 1-866-488-7386

Bizarre Ones

We are the bizarre ones.
We live on the edge of sanity.
We wear our crazy as bright, bold colors that scream into the night. We dance in the dazzlingly dare that is "difference".

A Narrative Rewritten

I wrote: Angry. Damaged. Alone. You replied: Raw. Honest. Real.
I saw: Beauty. Redefined. Vulnerable. It was: A narrative rewritten.

A Letter to my Molester *(written in 2015)*

Dear Asshole:
(I refuse to use your actual name because it sickens me). Your face makes me ill but try as I might, I cannot erase it from my memory. I still remember the smell of your rancid breath, the heat of your body, the tremble of your lips against mine. I wracked my brain for reasons why. Why did you do it? Why me? Why for so long?

I want you to know that I'm angry. Because of you I feel unworthy of real love. Because of you I fight to stay alive every single day. Because of you I have a deep seated fear of men, of physical intimacy, of emotional and physical vulnerability. Because of what you did and how you broke down my body and soul, I will never be the same.

You stole my fucking childhood. My innocence. My ability to feel safe and well loved. You picked me apart and made me believe I was unlovable except in your way. You made me feel like I was ugly and that I deserved to be humiliated and poorly treated.

I bear the labels "victim" and "survivor" because of your selfish hands. I know things I shouldn't know about touch, because of your depraved imagination. I never meant to be this person. I never wanted to be a survivor. They said "God doesn't give you more than you can handle..."

God has nothing to do with what you put me through. I may be stronger for it but I never wanted to be this strong. I want my innocence back. I want to go back to seeing the world as beautiful rather than full of creeps like you.

It makes me sick what you did to me. How you preyed on my naiveté and love for you as my brother. How you betrayed my trust and ruined relationships and friendships.

You got away with destroying me. No one believed me. You're so beloved and charming. The way you twist your words is outstanding. You've never shown the tiniest bit of remorse and now it makes no difference.

The statute of limitations on your crimes is up. And you knew I would never do that to the family. I hate all this anger and frustration I feel because I have to be a fucking island.

Depression--snippets from my personal blog (*August 10, 2014*)

I've heard it described as fibromyalgia of the heart. I can't express how accurate that is. It's like being in constant pain. Sometimes dull and throbbing. Other times sharp and exploding. However, similar to fibromyalgia, this is not a pain that others can see, nor can it be fully described to accuracy. Those who have it will understand.

As a writer, I am able to look back and track some of life's biggest moments. For me, many of my big moments have also been in direct correlation to a depressive episode or two. If living has taught me nothing, it's that there is a power in secrets and shame. That power is often malicious, malignant and misused by the wielder of the power. Thus, the sugar coating ends here. Two weekends ago, I tried to take my life. This is not the first time I tried nor my most serious attempt. What stopped me you might ask? Thoughts of friends and family? My cat insistently rubbing against my legs? A sudden realization that I did not want to not exist anymore? None of the above. Some may say fate, or a higher power; God. I reached out for help as a joke by calling a hotline, just to see what they would say. Let me pause here and just convey that when someone is seriously suicidal, words have the power to completely change that moment. In my case, the words were actually, truly unhelpful. But the amount of emotion and energy it took to wade through that tedious conversation was enough to plummet me into a deep exhaustion. I don't remember falling asleep, but when I awoke I no longer even had the energy to finish what I had started.

So I was back to my emotional fibromyalgia. Looking completely fine and "well" from the outside but in constant, incessant, unrelenting pain on the inside. If depression were an addiction I would be classified as a "functional addict". In the mental health field I am considered "resilient". This is somewhat of a blessing and a curse. Resiliency is the dream of every mental health provider who comes across a trauma survivor. You silently cheer when your "patient" or "client" has the internal reserves to overcome great adversity and still retain a semblance of normalcy and health. In my case, I am hugely independent, driven, intelligent, and somewhat sociable. Sounds great! I'm not an immediate crisis case or delinquent. However, this also means when I am actually in crisis, I appear simply stressed. My independent nature is so over-exaggerated that my life is in danger 95% of the time without anyone actually realizing that is the case. Add to that, I have trouble asking anyone for help. Suddenly resiliency is no longer the ideal standard.

My life is a long pattern of what I like to call "even" moods followed by increasingly intense depressive episodes and suicide attempts. It's so commonplace to me that at this point I forget how alarming this information can be for other people. I never want to scare anyone but explaining my reality to them so I often do so in small doses, with lots of protective language and hardly in full detail. In fact, this may be the most real account that I have ever expressed. Ironic, I chose the anonymity of a blog to be honest. In any case, I like to put things in writing when I want to remember or challenge myself. I have so many words trapped inside of me at this moment, but they are nonsensical. So I will end with this.

Depression is real. Depression hurts. If you know someone

with depression or you have it, be patient, especially with yourself. It's one of the most painful things in the world.

Hard

Life was hard. She used it to sharpen her edges and to cut like a knife. Nothing was stronger than her backbone.

Suicidal

Today I nearly killed myself.
I danced with death and put it back on the shelf. My skin aches for the prick of a knife.
I no longer want to live this life.
My feet fly toward the edge of that bridge with a fevered tempo. There is a voice telling me to let go.
Oh, how I long for that sweet slumber. To let the river take my soul asunder. Today the bridge. Tomorrow the knife.
Yesterday the pills. Every day an afterlife. Again and again I find this ledge.
Today the platform. Tomorrow the edge.

Tears
==

My face is wet with liquid pain,
That my heart has no clue how to contain. The thunderstorms of protest are over.
Now all that's left is gentle rain.

PART 2: HEALING

This section of the book was written while I was still in a very hurt place and hoped that healing would be possible. Almost 10 years later, I can look back and confidently say healing is possible and has taken place. Revisiting this book has been a way to measure just how far I have been able to come from a place I thought I would never escape.

Let's Be Honest--Life Lessons   (*Blog Entry December 28, 2012*)

1. I am my own worst enemy. No one poses more of a threat to my safety than I do.
2. Humans are just that; Humans.
3. Life is equal parts pain and pleasure.
4. Internal pain can be more life threatening than physical ailments.
5. Trauma has changed the way I view the world and how I build relationships.
6. The people who love you the most are the people who can hurt you the most.
7. The people you love the most are the people who will hurt you the most.
8. Vulnerability is the hardest thing in the world.
9. I have many beautiful parts.
10. I am loneliest in a room full of people because I know those people don't really know me.
11. I am not always as alone as I feel.
12. Not everyone deserves a second chance.
13. Whole-hearted people are the strongest people in the world.
14. Great risks may lead to great rewards.
15. Sometimes silence is golden, other times it is a cry for help.
16. Admitting you are not okay, is not admitting weakness.
17. Life is all about letting go.
18. Old habits do die hard.
19. I don't have to be 100% okay to take care of someone else.
20. Sometimes, loving someone means letting them hurt you, deeply.

21. Just because I can see it, does not mean other people can.
22. I am blessed.
23. I am selfish.
24. I am a risk-taker.
25. I am an artist.
26. I am wounded.
27. I am healing.
28. I am strong.
29. I am a survivor.

<u>Best</u>

I never said I would be good at this. I only ever said I would try my best.

Can't Love

I can't teach you to love.
I can't show you what I need. I can't make you stay here.
I can only watch you leave.

I can't teach you to love. I can't be who I am not. I can only do my best.
This is all I've got.

I can't teach you to love. I can't make this better. I can only take so much.
I wrote it down in a letter.

I can't teach you to love. I can barely love myself.
I wish we could have made this work. Rather than put love on the shelf.

Demons

My demons look a lot like you.

Fuck It
Fuck this. I quit. The end.

Go
Do not detour or pass Go.

Color
I am becoming a brand new color.

Liar
You are the most charming liar.

Love
I can't teach you to love.

Healing
Doesn't matter. It's over. Move on.

Fight
I would have fought for you.

Tell me
Keep telling me that I can't.

Nightmares
I have the most exquisite nightmares.

Come Inside

Come inside.
Get to know the quiet spaces of my soul. Listen to the whispers in the hall.
Take your shoes off and indulge in the music of my spirit.
Fall asleep listening to my dreams.
Come inside.

Part 3: HOPE

Original blog excerpt posted: January 4, 2023

I know my mother would also have been proud of me. Or, the me she thought I was. See, we had been estranged for most of my adult life and our relationship was tumultuous long before then.
But she was my mom. She was with me 24/7 365 for 21 years. And there was a person that she had gotten to know as me, but was not really who I am. I only started peeling back the layers of my identity in the past 5 or so years. I was clueless as to what my true self looked like. And now I know, but she never will.
My mom died December 2021. I've never really loved December/the holidays because of how
things went down in my house, but I never hated it more than the moment I got the news. I hadn't seen my mom in 8 years. We'd spoken on the phone at times before I asked for no more communication. Recently I've been having a lot of health issues (get ready for that post) and I needed familial information from her. This opened the door to us having a very frank and honest conversation. She apologized and acknowledged the harm done and while recognizing there is no way to make that go away, we agreed to attempt to form a different kind of relationship.
2 days after that conversation, she died. Boom. In an instant. She was gone before the

paramedics arrived according to my father. I still have trouble believing any of this is true and that she's really gone. I think because I hadn't seen her in so long, my last image of her is alive. And as much as I want to keep that, I also wish I had had the chance to say goodbye.

This past year has been so incredibly hard. There were some really, really enjoyable moments and there were moments when I couldn't breathe. I wish my mom had met me. The me I am today. BLACK, queer, non-binary and successful AF! And saying it loudly. I think she would like me to be unapologetically myself. Or at least, I'd like to think that.

Vulnerability

Throwing off perfection, Leaves only the messy bits.
The broken, tacky glued together, broken again parts. The smashed and shattered pieces of a life lived honestly. The frayed strips of an adventurous soul.
Faded colors of a genuine spirit. The beauty of vulnerability. A peculiar treasure.

Need

I need someone who makes me happy, the way you made me sad.
I need someone who takes time out to appreciate joy and the feeling of being glad. I need someone who breaks my walls instead of breaking my heart.
I need someone who sees my beauty, my life in my art. I need someone who knows the value of being true What I recognize that I truly need is the opposite of you.

Hold me

Hold me.
Would you please put your arms around me?
Let your hands meet at the center of my back. Squeeze my body tightly against yours. Hold me.
Share my warmth.
Feather kisses across my eyelids. Let me kiss your neck. Hold me.
Don't let me feel cold. Don't let me be alone. Hold me.

I am crying silent tears. I am so frightened.
Please, hold me.
Can you hear the words my heart is saying? Can you understand my sighs?
Can you feel the love in my eyes? Oh, baby. Please hold me.

The hours are going too fast.
In the morning we have to say goodbye.
If these are our last moments will you just hold me? We knew this moment would come.
But, before the sun rises, Just hold me.

I promise I'll never forget. I promise I'll always care. I know you won't.
But, please hold me.
Pretend like your heart beats for me the way mine does for you. Soothe my pain with your fingers.
Dispel my solitude with your hands.
Bind my bones back together with your arms. Hold me.

Do you know that to me this bed feels like home?
Do you know I replay these stolen moments when I am

alone? Oh, curse the sun!
Let this night last forever. Don't leave me.
But, if you must, first, please only hold me. We don't need words.
This is how we love. Limbs entangled.
Your chest against my back.
Sharing the twilight. You holding me.

"I Love You"--A Dream

I see you looking at me and I duck my head, lower my eyes. My heart is beating wildly but I am doing my best to appear calm. I glance up. You are still looking. Even more intently and suddenly you move. I know you are coming over but I glance away again, trying to hold back my feelings for one moment longer. I hear you settle in next to me and your hand slowly creeps over to find mine. I lock fingers with you in a desperate grip. You chuckle and I can't help but smile. This feeling is so electric every time.

Suddenly I am in your arms and tears come unbidden to my eyes. I can't help it. Standing here with you feels like coming home. You know that I am going to that place in my head where I ask myself if I deserve you or if you will leave. You tip my head back and answer slowly. "Yes", "No". Each word is spoken softly. Each word punctuated by an even softer kiss.

I sigh. I am melting from the inside out. This always happens when you kiss me. I can't hide when you kiss me. I am truly, wholly present and you see all of me. What's more is you love all of me. Over and over. Everyday. You choose to love me. That destroys me. It makes me feel so vulnerable. Yet I always feel safe. Because you know me, choose me, love me. I smile and whisper "I love you". One last squeeze and we return to the party. You never stop holding my hand.

Don't Get Used to Me

Please don't get used to me. Please don't find me boring.
Please find my clumsy ways endearing.
My whiskey eyes, alluring.
Please love the curl of my dark chocolate hair. The slender curve of my body.
Please kiss my eyes, my face, my lips and trace your name so lightly. Please ache to hold me every night and miss me when I'm gone.
Please call me when I'm feeling low and talk with me til dawn. Oh, lover please don't let me be.
Please don't go away.
Please don't ever get used to me. Just promise me, you'll stay.

Home

She longed to be loved.
She wished for a safe place, home. And It broke her heart.

Breathe

Tomorrow we die.
Today we learn how to shine. Each breath is a gift.

Alchemy

Never stop writing. Howling. Bleeding. Alchemizing. Making magic, love and beauty.

My art is my life and my life is my work. I write to live and live to write.

Words are the language of my soul and the music of my hands.

www.ingramcontent.com/pod-product-compliance
Lightning Source LLC
LaVergne TN
LVHW022001060526
838201LV00048B/1656